'I must go
Where the four winds blow
Where the spirit speaks to its own,
For now I am free
Like the wind I must be
And help the others home.'

WHEN BARRY LONG uttered these words, forty years ago, he had no idea of what was to come. Now we know – because his spiritual teaching has gone to the four corners of the earth, and he has fulfilled the mission of every spiritual master – by helping the others home. This place, eternity, our true home, is the cause of such longing that it famously inspires the mystic and the poet.

ALL HIS LIFE Barry Long has sought to express his passion for the truth, to say the unsayable and articulate the divine mysteries of life. This book is the expression of that mystic call and a song of praise to the source of all spiritual inspiration. It contains poems and verses he wrote privately from time to time in his personal journey home. So it's a unique testimony by a modern mystic. And yet, since the inspiration is absolutely impersonal, this is a book with the power to touch every reader who has ever known that same longing; who can hear the spirit speaking to its own.

Barry Long was born in 1926 and lives in New South Wales, Australia.

Also by Barry Long

A Prayer for Life: The Cause and Cure of Terrorism, War and
Human Suffering

The Way In: A Book of Self-Discovery

Making Love: Sexual Love the Divine Way

The Origins of Man and the Universe

Only Fear Dies

Meditation – A Foundation Course

Stillness Is The Way

Knowing Yourself

Wisdom and Where to Find It

Raising Children in Love, Justice and Truth

To Woman In Love

To Man In Truth

Audio Books

Start Meditating Now

A Journey in Consciousness

Seeing Through Death

Making Love

How To Live Joyously

BARRY LONG

Where the
SPIRIT
SPEAKS
TO ITS OWN

*The passion
of
spiritual
awakening*

BARRY LONG BOOKS

First published 2003

BARRY LONG BOOKS
BCM Box 876 London WC1N 3XX, UK
Box 5277, Gold Coast MC, Queensland 4217, Australia
6230 Wilshire Blvd – Suite 251, Los Angeles, Ca 90048, USA
www.barrylong.org   Email: info@barrylong.org

Cataloguing-In-Publication Data:
A catalogue record for this book is available from the British Library.
Library of Congress Catalog Card Number: 2002094478

ISBN 1 899324 16 X

Cover photo, Himalayas: Courtesy of Ashok Dilwali
Back cover photo is of Barry Long in 1982
Inside drawings: Andrew Hawdon

Printed by Kyodo Printing, Singapore

Contents

FOREWORD

Barry Long is one of the leading spiritual masters of
our times. As he went through the fire of God-realisation
he was compelled to express his new knowledge in
poetry and song, as other mystics have done down
the ages.

His collected poems are now published together
for the first time. They bear extraordinary testimony to
an imperative call of the spirit to say the unsayable,
articulate the elusive, refine and define the ever-finer

truth – to worship in words the wonder and mystery of our lives.

Some of the longer pieces are driven by a raw rhetoric and an urgent dialogue with the inner voice of truth, whereas the songs may be light of heart or poignant, anguished or sweet. But every line speaks of the collision between our limited personal lives and the utterly impersonal power which ultimately rules human destiny.

These writings open our ears to the 'silent song of life, a song within all things that be'. They urge us to listen, and to heed the call to fulfil our life's purpose.

Clive Tempest

INTO THE UNFATHOMABLE . . .

In forty years as a spiritual teacher I've been helped, loved and served by a great number of people around the world and in Australia. I've had a wonderful and extraordinary mystical life although in the early years of my transformation I recall declaring that I'd never forget the pain and suffering I'd had to go through. But I did. And by grace I was led somewhere into the unfathomable mystery of God or Life, and at the same time into that other divine mystery of true love between man and woman.

The poems that follow were written during three distinct phases of my spiritual life.

First are my songs written between the late 1950s and early 60s. Together with their introductions they describe much of my life during those radical early years.

The second section consists of the epic poems written in London in 1967 and describing the divine scheme and intelligence behind existence.

The third section comprises poems mostly written in the mid 1970s, with a sprinkling from later years and a few from the late 60s.

Songs

of

Life

The story of a man pinned like a butterfly by the spirit.

When the spirit started to enter my brain at around the age of 31, I expressed in song what was happening. Some people write poetry. For me, it was verse with melody. This was in the late 1950s and early 60s. I was no songwriter and no poet as far as I knew and certainly no singer.

Even so, the songs are something of a record of the extraordinary phenomenon of the spirit working in man. And perhaps when you read them they will help to clarify areas of your life.

The songs all came spontaneously and are printed here as I sang them from Sydney to the Himalayas, where they stopped.

The songs are the story of an ordinary family man, father of two young children, and of all unlikely people, a Sydney newspaper journalist about to be made an editor; a man who without warning found himself pinned inescapably like a butterfly by the spirit.

Moreover, the impetus, the needle five years into the process, was a woman.

Her name was Ann. And in a vision of her normal earthly form in the full light of day she revealed herself to me to be the divine spirit, God, in female form, the incomparable one, the Bhagavati. All this without Ann realising it or anyone else noticing. A sure recipe for delusion and disaster if ever there was one— and I knew it.

Bhagavati is an ancient Hindu word from the Sanskrit. I had read the word in passing, as you'd read the word 'goddess' without dwelling on it.
But Bhagavati and goddess, as I was shown, are not just words. They stand for the living reality of woman, the essence behind or inside every woman, the original Eve of the West. There is one Bhagavati and three billion women.

Every woman's longing is to realise this essence of her being, this divine She, and every man desires her beyond all else.

When the Bhagavati appeared to me, I was utterly astonished. I voiced my instant recognition of her as the

Lord and she replied, 'Of course it is I, there is no Ann. But I will not reveal this to anyone, nor will you be able to tell anyone. In this way I will have my way. But I promise you I will unite you with this love'. The promise of union was because I loved her as God, and in form, with excruciating devotion.

Today I am united with this love. The incoming spirit that the world and my own ignorant brain tried to dismiss as illusion, is now master here.

It took many years. I had to die for the essence of woman, the love of woman in several of her forms. But as was promised, it is done; I am one with the formless. Here is my song to the Bhagavati in human form from those very early days.

BHAGAVATI

*B*hagavati . . . Bhagavati . . .
Planted together by the eternal giver
Two willow trees
Dipped and sipped at the river of Life.
Bhagavati . . . Bhagavati . . .

Neither in the shadow of the other
And yet
Both intermingled like wind that has met
Each one alone
Though eternally bound
By the ground.

Bhagavati . . . Bhagavati . . .

When death the compassionate giver arrives
Both fall in
And die

Bhagavati . . . Bhagavati . . .

And man, isn't his essence God too? Yes. He is Bhagavat. He is spirit, God in male form. To see him, woman must also die for love by dying to her self. Once seen, she will never leave him, nor he her. Love of Bhagavati or Bhagavat is identical with love of Life, the living formless God of all. For love is simply life lived free of fear. So here's my song of life, written while the children prepared for school and I dressed for work, oblivious of what was coming.

MY FRIEND LIFE

My friend life is death and birth
My friend life is the whole wide earth.
My friend life is sorrow and a tear
But my friend life does not know fear.
All the people would drag me down
But not while my friend Life's around.
My friend Life is change and pain
But that's all part of my friend's game.
Play the game and it can be fun
Fight to win and the fun's all done.
My friend Life is an outstretched hand —
It's your friend, too, if you grab it, Man.

The love I am speaking of, the love of man and woman as Bhagavat and Bhagavati, is of course, Tantra. That most rare and ancient way to the realisation of God or consciousness in existence. Tantric love has become sex. Where Bhagavat or Bhagavati make physical love, there is no sex. The lovemaking is simply the making of God, for God is the consciousness of love. If you make love, you make God. If not, you're having sex and making trouble for yourself and the partner.

Sex is love at a distance. Sex is love in two bodies separated by excitement, fantasy or fear. So where does sex begin? Where does excitement begin? Where does fantasy or fear begin? What is the great divider?

THE PLACE OF THE SINKING HEART

The cry of the sinking heart
Is the sigh of the thinking heart
For if you think
Then you must drink
At the place of the sinking heart.

Your thought is but spawn of the past
Caught on memory's treacherous cast
And if you think
Then you must drink
At the place of the sinking heart.

My wife Betty was under awful pressure. Normal family living was increasingly difficult. I wanted the reality of life and yet all I could see was the falseness we were living as life. Not just us, but everyone I knew.

Even in those days I possessed a certainty of knowledge and I used it like a whip. I assailed friends, family, relatives, neighbours with the truth as I saw it. It was as though I were looking for someone to prove me wrong, to destroy me with greater knowledge. (I would have to wait another five years for that to happen, in London.)

Meanwhile, nobody had any answers.

As for Betty, I had no alternative to suggest except that our life together wasn't working. I could do nothing about it. I could not quit; I was surrendered. I was using the pain of the situation to die to myself. It would change when I had changed, that I knew. I also knew that Betty fought because she was unable to understand (until the end) what was happening.

Also, I was betraying her by not being honest with her about Ann. But that to me was a worldly interpretation which I could not identify with and remain surrendered to the divine will; for guilt is the opposite to surrender.

(Even so the unerring and relentless wheels of divine justice — Karma — the reckoning in terms of worldly actions irrespective of spiritual motives, were already grinding towards me.)

15

Betty never really complained or blamed me and never has, as far as I am concerned. Everyday I told her of the truth I was discovering. Sometimes she heard, but rarely until later, when it was time. She was there for me, to make it hard, as I was there for her. I wrote this for Betty to sing to herself. On the good days the four of us would sing it around the house.

(The Lord refered to in the poem is The Lord within, not any historical religious figure with a name.)

SAVE ME FROM MY SELF
For Betty

I knew him well
Or was he a stranger?
O Lord save me from my self.
A thing from hell
Or a straw from the manger?
O Lord save me from my self.

A devil says the world
And I have to agree
Then I recall the things he said to me
And my whole being cries 'stop this heresy'
O Lord save me from my self.

The words that he spoke
I can no longer remember
O Lord save me from my self.
But they sounded a hope
With a new kind of splendour
O Lord save me from my self.
I didn't hear a word with these ears of mine
And I still would have seen had I been born blind
He raised me beyond the world of my mind
O Lord save me from my self.

From the start of the spirit entering me, I was amazed at the blindness of humanity. I was amazed at everyone's unquestioning acceptance of the ceaseless, repetitious daily comings and goings, as life. Nothing changed. Nothing had changed. Everyone was born to die and weeping and worrying in between. No one seemed to think this unusual or even worth scrutinising. Yet, what could I do about it? It must be right even to be wrong.

THE STORY OF A MILLION YEARS

How do you write
The story of a million years?
How do you write
The story of a river of tears?
How do you write
The story of eternity?
How do you write
The mystery of you and me?

The whole world's agroaning and travailing in agony
Aweeping and afearing as it shuffles towards its destiny.
How do you write
The story of this tragic throng?
How do you write?
How do you write?
How can you right what's wrong?

You must not lose yourself in love or you'll suffer for nothing, like most do, when the object of love departs in time, as it must. You must hold to the purpose of love. Love's purpose is to burn you out, to remove the selfishness that suffers from love. Know that and you suffer rightly. I learned for the first time what it meant to give selflessly to the Beloved through Ann.

BELOVED WOMAN

$\mathscr{I}$ can't give you anything.
Every gift I give is the gift of him
Whose gift of love we share
Who's gift of love so very rare
Takes all the world can give
Even the will to live
Yet loses in the exchange.
This love beyond all space and time
Whispers in the heart
Though unpossessed
You are forever mine.

To Ann, looking into her eyes:

Sweet Death

Sweet death
Where the beginning lies
I see you in the blackness
Of my beloved's eyes.
Still, silent, you look out at me
End of becoming,
Oh sweet eternity.

I'd never really loved until I loved Ann. I had thought I loved. But the love of the Bhagavati is too big, too all consuming, to be contained for long in the personal love of a woman. And yet this divine love must come through the love of a woman, just as the love of the Bhagavat must come through woman's love of a man. Any personal love will be destroyed. This is the agony of great love, the destruction of the person, the personal. Love finally can only be of the whole, not of the part. Otherwise love degenerates into loneliness, fear, dependence, depression and mourning. Love is life, all of it.

MYSTIC LOVE

*A*nn
Oh mystic love
Oh soul that's knit with mine
You're everywhere
Ann.

The sky
The fulsome clouds
The wind that cools the day
You're everywhere
Ann.

With my love reflected everywhere like this, how could I ever complain of being alone or without her, even as, inevitably, she left me — breaking my human heart out of her love of me to make me strong. For the love of the beloved is the love of the principle of love, and that, at its source, is God. And the only purpose in God is for each of us, over time, to realise the truth.

So Ann departed in the flesh never to be seen again to this day by Barry Long. Aah the bitter cup. How bitter is the cup that man or woman must drink to cleanse their love of self, their selfish, personal love. How hard it is to not push the cup away, to not hold back from drinking. And how hard it is to ask for more, if it be necessary.

BITTER CUP

My cup was filled with happiness when I first met you
It overflowed with love and joy but you said adieu
I know now why all lovers choose
To have at least and then to lose
Bitter Cup
Fill it up
And let me drink again.

Take this bitter cup of mine
And fill it up again
Hand it back and let me drink
Then fill it up again
Fill it up, fill it up
Fill it up, fill it up
Fill it up, fill it up
Fill it up, fill it up
Fill it up
Bitter cup
And let me drink again.

To me, right suffering, although personal, meant glimpsing the profound purpose of it.

GETHSEMANE

In a garden, a man knelt praying
While nearby three others slept.
Pain and suffering he saw before him
But for the world, not self he wept.
Gethsemane, Gethsemane.
Garden of despair.

One day in 1962, Betty, I and the children were visiting my father. We were sitting around the kitchen table. An intense feeling of being crowded arose in me. I got up quickly and walked outside.

STAND BACK

Stand back, oh stand back
Stand back forever
Stand back, oh stand back
Stand back it's now or never.

I must go
Where the tall trees grow
Where the giants stand alone,
And there I will be
Made eternally free
For I am going home.

Stand back, oh stand back
Stand back forever
Stand back, oh stand back
Stand back it's now or never.

It was a catchy little tune and driving home we sang it together. None of us ever guessed the words were prophetic. Three years later I had left Betty, the children and just about all I'd acquired. I was living in the Himalayas in Northern India where Ann had left me. There, I passed through the illusion of death and realised immortality. At that moment I saw the truth of the words of the song. In front of me was a forest of tall pine trees covering the hillside. Behind me were the giants, the majestic peaks of the Himalayas, and inside me, I was freed, I was home. The second verse of the song came immediately. It was as prophetic as the first.

I must go
Where the four winds blow
Where the spirit speaks to its own,
For now I am free
Like the wind I must be
And help the others home.

Stand back, oh stand back
Stand back for ever
Stand back, oh stand back
Stand back it's now or never.

In India I used to look at the beautiful colours of the distant horizon and long within to be one with that beauty. No more. It was done. The beauty now was here, within me. However, the realisation of death or immortality is a beginning, not an end. The Master Consciousness within is still far beyond that. Death is merely the death of fear and fear is simply holding on to what is or what has been. When I let go of everything, particuarly my longing to be what I am not or where I am not, I am liberated from death. In India leading up to immortality the day came when I parted consciously from my egoic wilfulness — the doer, the chooser, the winner and the loser. Here's that song.

GOODBYE OLD FRIEND

Goodbye old friend
This is the end
For you and me
The path splits here.
You must know
It's time to go
Old friend, my fiercest foe
Farewell.

It once was fun
To think we'd done
To win and lose
Reject and choose.
But as the youth outgrows the toy
Dearest possession of the boy
We're through.

ME AND M'OLD SAHIB HAT*

In India there were also times of fun and humour

$\mathscr{I}$ drove across India in a Ford
Me and m'old sahib hat.
I climbed the Himalayas to find the Lord
Me and m'old sahib hat.
I sat in the winter sun and wrote a book
And the natives all laughed as they took a look
But how could I tell them I was still half cooked
Even in m'old sahib hat.

* What I call a sahib hat is a lightweight helmet-shaped topee made
of pith or cork, effective in the heat and popular among the British in
colonial India who were called 'sahibs' by the Indians.

THE DANCE OF MY BELOVED

Ann would sometimes dance for me

Dance, dance, dance for me
Swish your skirt, let your hair fall free
Stamp your heel and let me see
The dance of my beloved.

One of my earlier songs while still in Australia was a ballad called, 'Akubra'. In the song Akubra is an aboriginal girl and her tribe is camped in the Circular Quay area of Sydney Harbour where the first fleet of British settlers landed over 200 years ago. The story is geographical. It describes Akubra's nine-mile run to raise the alarm after seeing the ships sail through the Heads. This is a heroic tale of woman's strength to do as she must, as she sees it, without personal consideration. It is a tribute to the one-pointedness unto death of the Bhagavati in woman to reach the Bhagavat, her love.

AKUBRA

A ballad

Akubra was her name
Akubra was her tribe
They had their camp at Sydney cove on the southern
    harbour side.
The young chief was her sweetheart
And on this day of summer heat
From nine miles out at Watson's Bay she spied the
    British fleet.
White-eyed she watched them sail
Through the Heads a mile away
She had to warn her lover — run nine miles on a
    scorching day.

So she

Ran, ran, ran
Yes she, ran, ran, ran
Till her breath would hardly come
Yes she ran, ran, ran, to warn her man
Beneath the blazing sun.

Up the hill and along the top where the lighthouse
　　stands today
Past Vaucluse Heights and Convent Point and down to
　　old Rose Bay.
A backward glance, a muted cry, the ships had cleared
　　the bight
Swifter, swifter, fair Akubra
No rest for you in sight.

So she

Ran, ran, ran
Yes she, ran, ran, ran
Till her breath would hardly come
Yes she ran, ran, ran, to warn her man
Beneath that blazing sun.

Point Piper passed, through Double Bay down the
　　Yarranabee ramp
Rushcutters Bay, behind The Cross — at last her
　　lover's camp.
With choking words, she gasped the news as her man
　　ran to her side
She fell into his outstretched arms

And her tortured body died.
They buried her
By the cool Tank Stream, now called Macquarie Place
Where the ghosts of Akubra and her chief
Still sing of that desperate race.

Yes she, ran, ran, ran
Yes she, ran, ran, ran
Till her breath would hardly come
Yes she ran, ran, ran, to warn her man
Beneath the blazing sun.

Always a romantic in the love between man and woman, I wrote these two funny little songs in the early days in Australia. Today they may seem outdated. But I suspect the poignancy they describe hasn't really changed, that the young heart still cries out for someone to love just the same.

PRETTY GIRL, PRETTY BOY

Pretty girl, pretty girl,
Pretty girl, pretty girl.
Walkin' down the street
Pretty boy, pretty boy,
Pretty boy, pretty boy,
How they'd love to meet
'She's so pretty,'
'He's so handsome,'
Thoughts fly as they pass
'Too many dates to think about me,
Oh, my aching heart.'

Chance, chance, chance
Can't you help them
Luck, luck, luck
Take a hand
Love, love, love sear them sorely
Join them with your golden band.

Pretty boy, pretty boy,
Pretty boy, pretty boy

Walkin' down the street
Pretty boy, pretty boy
Pretty boy, pretty boy
Stumbles at her feet
'Gee, I'm sorry, gee, you're pretty
I'd like you to know
If you'll be my lovin' friend
I'll be your lovin' beau.'

Chance, chance, chance
Yes you've helped them
Luck, luck, luck
Now take a hand
Love, love, love
Sear them sorely
Join them with your golden band.

Pretty girl, pretty girl
Pretty girl, pretty girl
Smiles into his eyes
'Pretty boy, pretty boy
Pretty boy, pretty boy
M'heart has heard your cries
Take my hand, take my arm

Take my heart and then
You can be my lovin' beau
And I'll be your lovin' friend.'

Chance, chance, chance
Yes you've helped them
Luck, luck, luck
You took a hand
Love, love, love
You've seared them sorely
Now join them with your golden band.

How a Young Heart Cries

Standing on the corner
Standing on the corner
Waiting for the girls to pass.
Standing on the corner
Standing on the corner
Waiting with an aching heart.
This way and that way
That way and this way
Swishing skirts and hidden eyes
Please don't traduce us
Please introduce us
Oh, how a young heart cries.

Turn back the years
Remember when
Your own true heart
Craved a pretty friend
Standing on the corner
Standing on the corner
Waiting for the girls to pass.

EPIC POEMS

OF

TRUTH

I wrote these poems in 1967 while working as the makeup sub-editor with the Evening News in Fleet Street, London. And ironically they were scribbled in pencil on scores of sheets of copy paper amidst the noise and clamour of the composing room while dozens of typesetting machines chattered away and compositors called for me to cut stories to fit the pages. It was the days of hot-metal printing. You'll read a passing reference to 'editions yet to run' in the postscript to one of the poems.

I was 41. I'd arrived in London a year before after 15 months in India, having left my young family and career behind in Australia.

The first poem, The Star, was inspired by my love of an English woman, Julie, who later became my wife of 13 years before she died aged 40. That love was the catalyst of all the poems that follow.

THE STAR

Julie
I have found the place you are.
Julie
How could I miss you?
You are a star.
Foolish mind, cage of vision
Sees the light but not the star
Staggers at the beauty it imagines to be far.
Julie
You are a star.
No mind through glutton eye has ever seen a star
Just the light . . .
And many lights there are.
Then where is beauty?
In the star.
Where the star?
Where you are.
And where is that?
Glutton eye would see you as afar
Again the light
And not the star.

Julie

Where are you?

With every other star

In the beholder

I

That's where you are.

Only the stellar system referred to in that poem is profound and total enough to illustrate the possibilities of man and woman's love. The firmament of stars in fact is life's symbol of their potential. Each man and woman is a star in the making, each endeavouring in time to shine in the timeless mystery behind existence.

Love that does not begin to glimpse that the beauty of the beloved is actually within the beholder is earthbound and deathbound. Love that does begin to glimpse this is also doomed, but differently. Such love has now to go beyond the earth and its exclusive loving, into the awesome aloneness of deep space. There the love of my children becomes the love of any child; my mother, any mother; my people, all people; my life, all life; each moment of love determined by where I am and what I do — for where I the beholder am, is life. This inward journey into immortality is a self-consuming destruction of all previous personal love that — with beautiful motive but unsuspected selfishness — would endeavour to hold on emotionally to the person loved, denying them the inevitable destiny of becoming their own star.

The following poem, also entitled THE GLUTTON EYE, *was written for a man who was losing his wife: a good man, a man who detested violence, who hated war, who genuinely desired good for people.*

As often happens when an individual is ready to discover the truth of their self, the blow came within weeks of my speaking to him. All the new knowledge he had listened to and embraced as an exciting new hope for man, he now had to live and apply in his own disintegrating world.

This poem (which follows on immediately after THE STAR*) describes the inner battle the man must expect with the pigmy of ignorance that hides in every man and woman. In the poem, Life converses with the pigmy, then lectures, exhorts and encourages the man; the man in turn appeals to Life for help from time to time.*

This man's battle lasted 18 months. At its height he actually saw the 'cold blue pigmy', shrunken, cringing rat-like within himself, a living entity as real as any good man who ever smiled and said, 'Good morning'.

THE PIGMY

What is it then that sees the light?
Same glutton eye that sees all strife.
Behind the eye, what pleads for peace?
Aha, the simpering inner beast.
Considerate, smiling, gentle, kind
That's mine host the contented mind.
But spill one drop from its twisted tin cup
And watch the filthy mess erupt.
The pacifist he turns to war.
What for? There is no war.
Yes, there is, my friend, you see
Every war begins in me
Behind the glutton eye
Where every war is justified.

Pigmy   In me? Wait, you said above that I contained
             the star, your love.

Life   No, no, that can never be
             You are not I, your name is me.

Pigmy   I, me, what's the difference here?

Life   Me (you behind the glutton eye) is fear.

Pigmy   Me, fear? That is not true, I live a normal life
          like you.

Life   You do? Your normal life is pursuit of gain
         Your desire for possessions, respect, even to
               be loved
         Is all the same
         To the glutton eye.
         The desire for gain
         Is but a coin whose obverse side is pain.
         It is me who gains and therefore fears — to lose.
         You don't think so? Then come on, choose
         What will I take first
         Your mother, wife or child
         So that you, fearless, will sadly smile
         And valiantly say take on?
         Me never ever said take from me
         For me exists in what is mine
         And what is mine exists in time
         And time is me's mortality

Death.
And who is I that threatens so
To take the child, the mother, wife
And what's more does and will one day,
    I promise you —
But Life.

Man   Will it (tell me Life) take all of me
House, son and honour?
Great God, the finality of my mortality
Which is my last possession.
But here I've crossed the coin
Where gain is loss and my eternal pain.
Life, if I should surrender all of me
Will you be true
For I cannot see what can be left?

Life   My son, dear doubting son
Who would argue with a star
From the heights of your wooden box afar,
I give you what you want, your doubt.
You search for doubt then you will find it.
Take it, grow in it, drown in it.
Hold on to your mortality . . .

Wait, that is but My passion,

The cleansing storm

The passion of a star

Justified, as all passion must be

By love's desire

To show you who you are.

True, I will gain — another star

Not gain like doubting, quibbling me

Who'd dare to challenge unceasingly

And having found no chink

Gloss over his stupidity

And fluctuating ignominy

The strutting sire of infamy

Dwarf-giant

The cold-blue pigmy

Behind the glutton eye.

Give up! Give up! Or I will take

And when I take I always take a gain.

Man   A gain or again?

Life   Again is but the repetition of a gain — won or lost.

When no more gain is left the thing must die

And never be again.

Man can't complain
For how can anything that dies have been a gain?
Or come again?
Yes, I intend to take a gain unless you give Me
    what I want
Now
Not tomorrow
Now.

Man   What is that?

Life   You.
        You behind the glutton eye. That's what I want.
        Come out of him, come out and die.

Pigmy   You know the law, you made it Life
        I am your guardian of strife
        Without me there is no life.

Life   True, you are all strife
        But don't pretend to Me you're life.
        The noun comes first, you are the verb
        To live,
        God of the herd
        Whose slow and secret course I set.

59

Pigmy   That might be so but you know the rule
          I'll not come out
          I am no fool.

Life   Ho, ho, old certainty again. You're coming out of
          this one.

Pigmy   When?

Life   Look at you, once so fat and sleek
          You're sick and starved and shame-faced weak.

Pigmy   No Life, that is not so,
          Rough it's been, but I'll not go.
          I'm thin from slipping through the door
          But I get in.
          The law says he must give me up.
          Imagine giving up his suffering and sadness
          His last clinging to this madness.
          Just cross him once, you wait and see
          Raging and cursing he will be.

Life   Go on, that's why you're greyhound thin.
          You haven't been getting enough of him.

Pigmy Enough to stay.

Life On your way.
Whirl on, small hurricane of desire
Pattern of all mixing
Forming
Twirling
Stirring
Like the sugared tea.
Whirl on and make your thousand million bodies
One by one,
Through which you step to Me
Finally shed of nought but clinging in the whirl
Of world
Where clinging is not necessary
Yet your necessity
Your poverty
Your ignorance of Me.
Express
Impress
Compress
Divest
And gather mass.
That is how all stars are formed

The heaven's and the heavenly.
A whirling whisp of My desire
The gathering of dust
The first of lust
For what lacks mass must cling.
A million years
The spin begins and in the centre knowing heat
Destroys the fears
(Essence of primordial tears)
And lust is outgrown
A baby body unable to contain
The energy of growing man
Or gathering star.
You see, all things are good to be
And what is bad is but a shedding
Of what you had,
The outer lust, your necessity
Before you knew all comes from Me
Your mass.
Bad is only what you are
The distance from your own star.

My Son,
The task ahead you have not had before

(It was I who held the closing door)
But now you must stand on your own,
Not alone, for I am always near,
Slay him, the pigmy, deny the beast his home —
The toughest blade you'll ever hone.
I do not ask this of the stone
The metal, tree or dog,
Or even of man born of womb
But of My Man, Man born of his own tomb
Where you are, the crucible of every star.
Remember as you slash and fight
Or tremble in the frightening night
To keep at bay this cunning mite
Who knows no rules like you, the knight,
Except the rule of spite
And hate
And anger
And remorse.
The last the worst
The curse
Of doubt posing as humility.
Remember
As dear as the unconscious things are to Me
(And all things I hold upon my knee)

There's none I love more dearly, none
Than you My beloved beamish son.
So let the battle now begin
The battle only a Man can win.

Man   Wait! Life! I am not clear,
       My opponent is not here.

Life   That is the battle, My Son
       To recognise him when he comes.
       No ordinary foe is he
       He'll even come disguised as Me!

Man   Good god, am I to fight a dream
       An enemy that can't be seen
       But comes disguised as Life itself
       How can I guard against such stealth?

Life   The trumpet has already blown
       Life pulses in the seed Life's sown
       Life never sows the seed until it's time.
       Your sword and lance I sharpened
       While you slept
       Your armour you hammered yourself

While you wept.
You are ready.
The battle must begin.
How long it rages will not depend on him.

Man   I understand now, Life,
If I am worthy it is my right
This final fight.
And one thing more I see,
My cries for peace were not of me,
What I demand is victory!

One word, dear Life, to carry in my heart
If the fight be long, perhaps to light the path.

Life   I sent My stars to tutor you
One said obedience will get you through.

Man   Obedience, what to?

Life   He told you never to contain, Me, Life
In anything so vain
As one thing.
When you cling to something of your own

You overlook Me as you would a stone
You exclude Me
And give a home to the pigmy.
You understand? Then obey.

Do you look upon your son
And see in him everyone
Who, like you, must one day face this test of Life
To put an end to pigmy strife
Not forgetting My special choice
That your son is there to hear your voice.
For what is love but need
A changing thing,
But not so, greed.
Rigid does the pigmy hold.

You say you do not need the books
And they may not be your way just now.
But know I speak through knowledge
The only comprehending thing,
Whether it be in living
(The home of pigmy strife)
Or in My realm, free non-containing Life
Through My instruments I speak.

Can I speak to man through a tree, a dog?
Of course I speak through them
But what is the knowledge of?
You say life.
No, a phantom knowledge there I give
The beauty of the will to live
As a dog or as a tree.
But what of man which is but Me
In My highest longing?
I speak through knowledge
And in ten thousand years
Where is that knowledge kept but in the silent ears
Of books.
For if you die tomorrow
What will you leave
For those who follow?
Little but a crying need
Your incomplete, unyielding greed.
Through whom will I speak then?
Your ghost?
Great god, he'll know no more than you before.
Wake up my son, the books are Me
My ever-living testimony
That there is hope

And not just you
For those who follow to turn to.

Watch out!
The pigmy comes.
Great God, his first guise is you've won.

The postscript . . .

Learn the secrets of this poem My Son
Written between editions still to run
Not in a cave
But in the sun
In the midst of life where the race is won.
And he who wrote it often had to pause
To sob, yes sob, and weep because
His finest straining chords
Could not contain the beauty on which I came
Through his pure heart
Dear, dear pure heart
Without the like of which I would be voiceless
In a pigmy world
Where all is shouting

And doubting
Behind the glutton eye.

You say you hear My hum in nature.
You do.
It is My silent song for the earless things
That have just begun to run.
None hears it who is not very close to Me
For it is a song within all things that be.
The earless ones could not go on without my hum.
You might recognise it
Listen now
The word is
Commmmmmmmmmmmmmmmmmmmmmmme.
But it's not enough for you, My Son,
Not enough for the final run.

ANNE OF THE TWINKLING I

For Anne, an Irish girl and Julie's best friend at the time

$\mathscr{A}$nne

Of the twinkling I

That shines above the glutton eye in you,

Another gathering star,

Lean on Me

Learn of Me

And mine.

My poem is for you

Too

As my poems are for everyone

To grasp unto themselves what is their own

For what you grasp in them is Me.

And if 5,000 grasp the same small portion

All amply fed will be.

Thus is the mystery

Of how I fed them by the sea

And later in their ecstasy

They saw me walk upon the water

And one of them

Did the same

Until he thought

And sank in his own doubt.

I pulled him out.

I loved him.

Take all you can

Anne

Of the twinkling I.

Woman's perception is different to man's. So her way is different. Woman is more intuitive, more superficial in her attachments, more able to forgo and forebear when the outer crust is penetrated.

Woman is less habitual than man. Her habit grooves are shallower because she has more love in her. Not the surface love that appears in most and that clings or even serves, but the unconscious love that destroys, that plays across her own habit grooves keeping them shallow and weakened.

This is the same unpredictable love that draws, weakens and destroys habitual man. It is the thing in woman he says he cannot understand. It is woman's forgetfulness, which is why she is protected by a natural intuition and unreasonable understanding. It is woman's flightiness, her tendency towards unreliability, irresponsibility and caprice, all elements of destruction of her own habit and man's expectations — all searing impersonal love. When woman is made perfect and is all this love, she is uncontainable.

THE WAY OF WOMAN

*I*f you look at My creation
You will see it stands upon the principle of opposites
Yes and no
Stop and go
Which in My higher throes
I present as male and female
And finally
As man and woman.
The way of yes can never be the way of no
Although
In the result they can achieve the same by different ways.
In element
Their time is spent in struggling
(Another word for argument)
To be united
Along their facing semi-circle paths.
But what man and woman fail to see
Is that
This cannot really be
Until the end
Where the circle is complete

The circle of eternity
Where opposites mix to unity
The meeting place of she and he
The end of the equation
Where there is nothing
Only Me.
I am you
Split in two.
That is the only agony.

From that, you will see
The way of woman cannot be
The way of man
To Me.

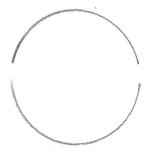

With the same instrument I prescribe the arcs
A perfect circle
Two different parts
Like down must struggle to be up
But up can fall.
(We are at the edge of all
Where words begin to fail
And understanding must prevail.)
Still, I go on.
My man must fight like a gallant knight
My woman must fight, too
But the fight of each is a different fight
Like yes and no.

My woman must fight to reach the lists
For only the noble can enter
Just as the knight must have slayed the best
To earn the right
To carry the glory of the final fight.
Hers is just a different role.
She must sit passive
(Though her body may tremble)
And watch the inner battle
Giving strength with her different strength

Refusing to scream

Or turn her eyes

(For that here would be ignoble).

It is not a knight outside her

She sees fight.

To imagine that is to see a light

With the glutton eye.

The fight is still within her.

She knows her knight

Don't you?

Think back to your first sight of him

As a child

A dream of innocence

Obscured by common sense

Restored by inner sense.

In every woman is her knight.

Her task is to be still, not join the fight

For that would be to doubt her champion

Her love.

A noble woman she must be

Steadfast

Worthy.

Every man is his own knight
And his task is to fight
The demon pigmy.

That is the secret of My woman and My man.
I know
Because I am the point of unity.

The poem that follows also was inspired by Julie who at the time was still leaving her husband. One evening she ran out of their house and down the street into my arms, refusing to compromise with fear of what people would think. In her action I saw life's infinite appeal — its refusal to compromise with death, destruction or society's notions of right and wrong.

People fear because they cannot face the fact of life's infinite destruction. Fear is anxious caring. Life does not care and yet it cares beyond all caring for it destroys and rampages only so that its infinite play of life may continue.

Can man and woman live like life? Can they stop fearing and anxiously caring?

Can they destroy their fears and notions every moment like life destroys its creations, and begin new and fresh with every moment?

Can they cease to compromise, not with others, but with their fears of what people will say or think, for apart from tomorrow, this is perhaps the most virulent fear?

Can man and woman never again look back with sorrow or regret on what they have done and so cease compromising with their imagination, guilt and excuses?

When compromise with fear ceases, caring turns to love.

WILD WILD, WILD *WILD* LIFE

Wild wild
Wild *wild* Julie.
Wild streaming hair
Wild breathlessness
Wild girl
Wild deathlessness
End of compromise
End of all that dies
Birth of wild wild
Purpose
And wild *wild* life.

Wild storm
Wild flood
Wild gushing lava
Flashing
Splashing
Crashing
Smashing through men's lovely gardens
While laughing wild *wild* laughter.

Wild forest fire

Roasting

Toasting

Wild *wild* agony

Hear you not the poignant cries

Of innocent suffering man

Of crackling hide and flesh

Of fledglings in the nest

Of slithering, withering, terrified scales

And flaming, running furry things

All that burn

With the terrible smell of spitting grease,

Or the nose-sweet fragrance of sizzling sap,

The blood and grease of trees?

Hear you not this misery?

Wild tearing teeth of the vicious shark
Wild blood that gushes from the bayoneted heart
Wild first prize carcass on the butcher's hook
Wild butcher of the butcher
Wild *wild* butcher
Of men and things.
Hear you not this misery?

Wild grabbing grave
Wild tiny, shiny casket
Container of another lovely garden
Ruined! Spoiled!
Gone forever.
You hear?
Finished!
The loving hope of a man and woman
Ended
In a tiny
Stricken
Cotton-wool stuffed body
With combed hair,
Stranded now in the stream of time
Every second more behind.
Grief, thief,

Torturing, unbearable grief.

How can there be a God when such things be?

Hear you not this misery?

Misery?

I hear no misery

I hear

Thirsting

Bursting

Wild *wild* Life,

An ever surging harmony

A sound of throbbing majesty

A choir of all the things that be

One-throated voice that soars to Me

And pleases Me,

The song of songs

The song of wild *wild* Life,

My song.

Hear you not my song?

Life, My all-containing orchestra,

Is a million swirling galaxies

(And the space between),

Each one a player

Whose awesome hands
Hold a million instruments
The flaring suns
That breathe and beat the energy of Life into the bars
That for you, earth man,
Are the earth
And the spinning, gathering planets,
Tomorrow's stars.

What is man in My timeless score?

In one birth
He is but one vibration
In the pitch
Of one note,
A minor chord,
A stroking
Sad, lamenting chord
That gives My song its wondrous tenderness
As the salt gives gay life to the sea.

Would you deny my song its ecstasy?
Of course you would
If you could

But you cannot.

Is that your destiny?

No.
I
Am your destiny.
But you are not yourself
Not yet.

How can you hear the song
While you are a part of it?
The player hits the note
And you,
My earth man
Jump, vibrate.
But let us say you don't.
Let us say you do what you do
But keep your equanimity
And watch the others jump.
What then?

By God
You'll feel the pain

As though you'd stuck your grease-thick hand in flame

And held it there.

The grease will burn

And so will you

With all the agony of the forest fire

The misery of crossed desire

The grief of the grabbing grave.

But

If you are worthy

You'll stand steadfast

With the terrible strength of the unyielding brave.

And suddenly

Indescribably

Consciously

Undeniably

You'll pass right through your agony

As though it were a barrier

That had imprisoned you

In a matchbox world.

There

Before your new innocent vision

Life unveils its best kept secret —

There is no death.

Still in the body

You clearly see

(More clearly than the nearest tree)

You've dropped forever the old accustomed form

You know you've been reborn.

Raised from the dead

Made a wilder, wider part

Of wild *wild* life

A part

That now lifts its voice and cries

Exultingly —

I am a part of everlasting life

I am all things

And all things are in Me

I am wild *wild* life

I am.

The trembling vibration

The last and highest in the pitch

Has now become the note

A complete identity

That stands above its burned-out discarded self

An immortal piece of wild *wild* purpose.

What have you lost that caused such pain?

You look back and smile, incredibly —

Nothing
Not one thing
You would want returned.
What have you gained?
Everything.
What else can I am gain?
Why did it hurt so much?
Ah,
That is life's mystery
That only the brave can see
Who dare to die for Me
In Me
Unto themselves
And go on dying.
There is no death
Just a dying to what you were before
An expendable reaction
To the closing door that closes
On nothing.

Are all men capable of such sacrifice?

No.
Not until they are ready.

Not until the final life.

I told you, man has many births

Many, many returns to earth.

But men get the foolish notion that what returns is them

This thing

Which today by anger caused commotion

Which by swelling pride and argument

Justified and preserved its individuality

Or even contentedly did nothing

But what it imagined to be its duty

To something outside itself

Outside its self-discovery.

That thing

Never ever returns.

Still, it has its heaven

For My justice provides a heaven for everything I have
    created.

But eventually, it dies.

True immortality is earned

By annihilating effort

In this life

Not contented, imagined duty

Outside yourself.

Ever was it thus

Ever shall it be.

Those who drop the body
Or die, as it is known,
Go on
For there is no death in My creation
Only birth.
Their death changes nothing
Except the domain
Which again is but a finer rendition of the earth
Where,
To their heavenly delight
Freed of day and night
Freed of the body's fright
And heaviness
They create like gods
The fulfilment of every wish.
Every gain they can imagine
Is theirs,
A chocolate shop world
Of untellable gorging and unspeakable bliss
For My ever-desiring children.
But it is not enough
Paradise is not enough

For my children of the earth

Who still cling through their unbirth

To what they imagine they left behind

Their undying,

Their individuality.

Filled with filling

They crave again for the challenge of living

For the roar of opposition

And strife

Where a man can gain something to hold in his hand

And keep it if he can

Hold it up for the world to see

And cry

Look at me

This is mine and mine alone,

And see envy

On another's face

And feel pride.

Not wave a wand as in fairyland

Where every wish comes true.

What sort of heaven is that

That gives it to every man too

And denies him

(Ah the sweetness of the thought)

Man's desire for power
Over man
And not himself.

So he returns
And in returning dies to his knowing
Of what he was before
(But not to his understanding
The honey in the unseen hive)
And he is reborn
Into a new fresh flesh
Striving form
Another tiny body
Another curious
Furious
Spurious
Personality,
Another life
To express another fragment
Of the world's desires
As yet unsatisfied by the understanding
Of gain not worth the pain
And time-robbed triumph.
It will not be a happy life

No matter how he tries

For already in his heaven

He has rejected all

For which he strives.

Except power,

An imagined gain that dies with him

Yet allows My game to continue.

Power

Is the subtle emanation

That appears in My creation

With the first possession

The knowing of individuality

Which begins with sense-feeling

Heightens with hearing

And separates completely

With seeing

Giving birth

(So neatly)

To me and mine

And thee and thine

And striving plants

And battling ants

And snapping dogs

And proud
Insulted
Men
Who go to war
To defend
The cause of war.

Only in such stupidity
Could I keep all from Me.

Living
(The death of life)
Is what earth man thinks he wants
Except sometimes
Thwarted by loss
He will imagine
He wishes he were dead.

Too soon to die
He recovers and thrives
The death-wish buried in a new desire
Until one day
The body aged and failing through the battering
Mercifully dies.

And he,
Changed again,
Sojourns in that heaven of his own making
Oblivious to his previous stay
And eventually
Living for the day
To return to his beloved earth
To try again.
Living is relationship
One to the other
The source of imagined power.
Life is being
Complete in itself.

The thing that goes on in earth man,
The thing that recurs and will not die
That fights the annihilating love of God
Yet continues My wild wild purpose there
Is ignorant desire for individuality
The opposite principle of unity
(If such a thing could be)
The fighting for duality
That even turns his heaven into hell
The principle of me and mine

That what he fights for is not thine
That mine is everything he can conquer
Outside himself.
For if he looked within
He would die
Of his own emptiness
And find a heaven
Worthy of man not bound by earth.
Such valiant men (and women)
Find their heaven in Me
Beyond eternity
Beyond cupidity and its stupidity
Yet within this body-being
And not in some far off imagined place.

Now

In the beginning is the word
Now
The word is made flesh
Now
You are born
Now
You are
Now
You die
Now
Yesterday was not or it would be
Now
See this and you are immortal
Now.

Man, The Thinking Piece of Sand

*E*arth man,
My death and birth man,
Knower of all but yourself,
You are trapped in a terrible illusion
That begins with the conclusion you are the body.
It is not so but you do not know
Any more than you can stay and go.
Because you do not know or go
Now.
One day you will and when, it will be
Now
Not then.

Man lives for knowledge
His life is the pursuit of knowledge
He is knowledge
Borne on an ache for knowledge,
A struggling pain to know.
Nothing else.
You recognise yourself?
No, you are too busy with the book

Too identified to pause and see who is the reader.

Man's life quest for money or success
To own a house or to possess anything outside himself
Is a striving
Not for the object but for the knowledge it is his.
He can never own the thing,
Child, house, car or diamond ring. It is his body's.
His sole gain is the knowledge
And that only to his satisfaction
Itself a mere contraction of his fluctuating knowledge.

A message says your child is dead.
What weeps?
The head.
But whence this pain
This gobbling agony of loss
This nothingness
This unbodyness
This phantom cross that holds you in a nailed embrace
So tight
You cannot even turn away your poor contorted face
But must bear on

As the hapless fox must run on and make the chase?

Whatever happened to cause such grief?

Nothing changed except you gained the knowledge you
 had lost your child.
And bright day became a suffocating night of grief and
 sobbing.
But wait! It was all a terrible mistake.
The child is unharmed.
Now blackness turns to brightest day
Thank God, you pray,
Yet nothing changed
Except you gained the knowledge your child was safe.
Without moving from your chair
Without one fact changing anywhere
You floundered in despair and soared to the heights of joy.

Is this the shifting sand
On which your happiness and suffering stand?
I'm afraid it is
Earth man,

While you abide outside.

Tell me Life, where is Inside?
Your words are honey to an emptiness in me,
Drips of golden sweetness falling where there is no tongue
An unlistening ear
That cannot hear above the thundering of its own desire
    for more.
I hear a silence
A soundless nearness
An unuttered answer to an unuttered cry
That delights me
Invites me
Forever to imbibe if only I can find the hive, the
    honey hoard.
Tell me Life, where is Inside?

Such longing, such loving savouring of My words
Is a thirst
A need from Inside
And shows much honey already in the hive.

This honey that man craves and saves from life to life
Is understanding.

And like the bee, he produces it from nectar,

His knowledge, gathered from each life's tree.

Knowledge is as useless to man as nectar to the bee

Unless he swallow it

And digest it

In the pulsing, transforming fire of his anatomy

And gives it up,

Not like a stream of undigested vomit

Of opinions and information

Of gorged nectar or knowledge stuffed from the
   wrong tree,

But as an emanation

A sparkling fermentation

A total confirmation of himself

A wisp of honeyed breath

A flowing, crystallised essence spreading where it may,

Not just a giving

But a living, sickness-need to bleed

Understanding.

Inside (this place you seek)

Is man's immortal centre

The treasure-house of his anatomy

A body-drossing furnace where My fiery alchemy

Turns his knowledge into gold.
How, I will now unfold.

But first, understand, that in going on
You enter another world
Where one life's knowledge is not enough to glimpse
all life's plan.
Hereon, knowledge falters,
Doubts because it cannot prove because of insufficient
knowledge —
A vicious circle even the cleverest cannot move beyond —
Unless there is sufficient honey in the hive.
Here begins in depth the realm of understanding
The subtle comprehension that goes beyond the word
And answers yes, yes, yes, to what is true
Not knowing why
Not knowing that it even knew.
That is the treasure-house, the sacred store in you.

Who am I?
I
Who come to you through this man mind and its
knowledge
On the pain dusted wings of his understanding,

Transcend knowledge. Where knowledge ends, I am.

To your comprehension I am nothing.

(Not even a new dimension, for that is something.)

At the end of everything that can be known am I —

The unknowable.

So do not look for Me, as such, in your mighty universe —

It is the death of Me,

The source of all mind knowledge,

Its infinity,

Which inexplicably

Exasperatingly

Automatically expands

At the same rate as man or mind discovers or understands

Any part of it.

A wonderful mystery.

All out there is knowledge

Nothing is the other way in the opposite direction

Away from the reflection

Inside the seer

The knower

You,

And it begins with the question

Who am I (you) who looks at the moon or sky for

    God or I?

And ends with the correct answer.

I am the Transcendental,
Creator of the Universe whose scheme I hold in imagery,
A sort of everlasting idea-mould that form and fate
     must follow,
A giant staircase of inflexible dreamstuff,
A maelstrom of relationship
A cataclysmic catastrophe of imbalance and harmony
From grit to star to man and all between.
Thus does man sense perfection as the ideal.
But imagery,
As he knows from his own imagination,
Is a pointless recreation, unless expressed in something
     sensed or seen by other men
A medium beween his idea and them.
So I created matter.

Oh, what illusion
Oh, what magnificent confusion I have created out
     of matter.
Man has never found a piece of it
Though he burrows, boils, splits and smashes
As is his norm.

All he can produce is form
The phenomenon of matter and My idea,
A trinity whose synthesis appears as structure.

First knowable structure is the universe,
Embracing structure of all structures
Which are but forms or parts of it
As a brick is a form of the house
And together, with all the other forms, forms the
Structure of the house.
Yet,
Brick and man are structures in themselves
Formed of form down to the atom
Another structure formed of form,
Of proton
Neutron
Electron,
Again when looked upon still structures composed of
    more vanishing form,
Of photon
And meson, the seeming end of form
Beginning of the abstract, nothing moving along a track
A wave
Form in motion

A tantalising non-going commotion of formless energy
Nearest yet to nothing
Nearest yet to Me.
Yet,
This outer world, your universe,
Itself is but a form of my unerring justice
(A mighty abstract house or structure of many mansions)
Which, as universal law, insists, all form must serve a
    greater form above
As each is served by a lesser form below —
So that
What is above is yet below, and that below is yet above
A choiceless serving, a giving, each form of itself to
    the greater —
Which is universal love.

This is my giant staircase where all things have
    their place
Grouped in ascending steps of structure
So that the lowest form contained within the lowest step
(And the order of things is My secret)
Leads ever up to Me,
A staircase of knowing to the end of
    knowledge-structure,

Eternity,

Which, Great God, is but a form of Me

Who am but another structure

Called infinity.

A marvellous, static, idea had I created,

But dead,

Lacking the ring of footsteps

Of movement,

Yes, of improvement.

But what could be improved in such a perfect work?

Knowledge.

Knowledge of what?

Surely not knowledge of the whole staircase of creation

Where one step alone is infinite formation

An inflammation of information

A self expanding creation of the desire to know?

How could such knowing ever be encompassed by a mind?

It cannot.

That is the outward knowing mindtrap I have laid

To keep things going, to divert and delay

And make the winner worthy of My accolade for

    right discrimination

In knowing what is worth knowing,

Where he is going,

Inside or out,

Towards or away.

And if man in his not knowing would enquire

Whether this means he no longer should aspire to

    reach the planets

(The outward going universal way)

Then he must be answered thus:

Man will never reach the planets

Though his body and his knowing may

And on that day it will be now not then.

To look with awe and wonder through those body eyes

At the pristine purity of My universe

Is an offering to Me

But to corrupt such wonderment

With thought

Or to smile triumphant

Is mistaking this new corner of his burrow for the prize.

Poised in the structure of My imagery

All things ever to be

I held suspended in a glass-cased frozen wonderness.

Into it I breathed a fire

Desire

The only fire

And all began to stir and move

Each form along its eternal groove

Of restlessness

Of discontent

Of sighing

Of trying to change

By accumulating, holding and shedding.

But form can never ever change

Outside the millennial shifting range fixed by Me

Except to boil

Or churn

Or tumble like the sea

In a fury of froth and seeming change

Under the spasm of the formless wave that having

    passed leaves sea behind

Untouched

Unchanged

Serene

Waiting to churn again.

So, by waves of energy, packages of My desire,

Is the sea of matter churned into brief droplets of form —

Of men and grit and stars and things.
For sand is sand in the beginning that never was
And man is man in the end that never can be
And each has its place by necessity
(Like the unending birth of the lemon tree)
In the great staircase of life.

Where stands man, the thinking piece of sand?
Last knowing structure
He begins with mind a million years below Me,
A befogged
Fearing
Sneering arrogance,
Not an ape as it is sometimes said

For the ape does not dread the future moment
Nor cling to guile and imagined cleverness to
     act outside itself.
Ape acts as ape.
And the highest form is highest knowing Man
The subtlest, purest, emanation of matter wherever
     he stand
With his precious knowledge of who He is.
Man alone has this capability
This fertility of maturity to flower for Me
In the spring of his vacuity.
It is his function, his unsparing service to the creation,
And when attained
He disappears into it and remains as its beauty
The hope of all behind.
Each man and woman is embarked upon this
     irresistible course
Treading life experience with shoes of birth and death,
Altogether, a shuffling pilgrim chain,
Some ahead, some behind
All blind, until the end, to the great purpose,
The last self-knowledge
That each must reach by gradual diminution
A creeping execution of himself

Of his not-knowing or knowing what is not,
Which he resists,
God, how he resists this slaying of his ignorance
From which his final phoenix innocence arises
Knowing nought
Yet knowing all
In I am.
What is this desire, this fire, that climbs My staircase?
It is not form, not body,
For the climber cannot be the climbed.
Form, as a continuum, a species or class, barely
    moves at all,
And as a shortlived individual expression
Jumps up and down in the one place
As the keyboard note can never hope to move from its
    allotted space
Or hold the formless tune that dances gaily past.
Who climbs My staircase?
I do. I as you, looking through those window eyes.
I, the knower, I climb the staircase.
Not I, the Transcendental, but I My lesser I
Who knows and is only what it knows.

As the persisting man outdone in argument

Displays his knowledge by his ignorance

And dictates his own assembly of those who find
    him wise

Or share his understanding

So lesser I, by what I know, choose my place in form

On My great staircase.

Lesser I is simply me as My creation

(Which could be said to be my own negation)

Me hiding from Myself

In escalating depths of not-knowing ignorance

In all the forms of stone, metal, plant and flesh.

Thus: I am in all things and all things are in Me.

Yet I who hide hide not in the form you see

But in the matter in between —

Its mystery.

Immersed and identified with my own creation

I lose the knowledge of who I really am

And the only escape is to know myself.

So, why does man desire to know anything outside
    himself?

To follow this, he has to rise above his arrogance

And see mankind as filling only a step or place

With no exclusiveness

Except

The system where he is, is moving at a faster pace

As it does the higher the Climber climbs.

This spiral of accelerating desire

At a point in living organism displays its fire as outer or
    surface mind

Then faster further on, as spreading intellect, until,

The ever-quickening rate produces higher abstract
    states or worlds

Where intelligence as concept fails

To indicate anything intelligible to the mind.

For example:

When nothing consciously experiences nothing as the
    beginning of everything.

Because nothing is the end of universal knowledge and
    desire

Mind is too low, too slow, to understand

And runs off in speculation, argues or demands elaboration.

Such a paradox is either pretension or the hope of men

For if true, it must mean something is beyond the
    mind that comprehends.

Man's position as a species is impersonal,

Just another village through which My climber has to pass,

And it is in separation, in standing back, in
    non-identification
With his personality (to begin with)
That frees him to climb on
To the last towering obstacle
The unthinkable
The logically insurmountable
The unassailable
The unscaleable
The Everest mountain of man's judging and opinions —
His mind.

Ridiculous, is mind's judgment of such a precious truth.
No man has ever gone beyond the mind, says mind,
Not understanding that no *mind* has ever gone beyond
    the mind
And never will.
For mind is penultimate form, and stays forever where
    it is
In the staircase to be climbed
By My unknowable knower.

Of course it is Mankind who climbs My staircase
But not the man or woman you know now

Not earth man who rests.
My Man, only a million years ago was a million
    fragments of all below,
Of stone, of sea, of cloud
That ever-discontented with partial knowing could
    not rest
And struggled ever on and up
Leaving stone and sea and cloud behind.
Until in panting unity, met and fused,
Forming universal mind,
Containing structure of all the glimmerings of
    self-consciousness
In the plant and worm and bird and beast
Below man.
Is that not your history too?
Yes. But nothing is yours until you know it.

Each man exists in My imagery,
So, essentially and individually, he is true and deathless
But what appears or manifests on earth
Is a natural, lower, slower, emanation
A blurred or distorted representation
Yet still bearing similarity
(According to its transparency and proximity)

To the essence it reflects.

After body, first manifestation in man is personality,

Then his knowledge and last his desire.

Put the other way,

Man first desires through his knowledge

(Being unable to desire anything he does not know)

And then tries to arrange its satisfaction through the
play of personality,

The phenomenal product of desire and wrong
knowledge —

Sham man

Which, like the sham coin, even to be sham must be
similar to the original.

Personality is the offspring of personal mind

Spawned of the conflict between the Climber and
the climbed.

Personality, in earth man, is corrupted individuality.

Or,

Earth man's individuality is corrupted personality.

Remove the corruption and what remains is purity

Of personality and individuality — man acting as he is.

The corruption is in the personality unconsciously and
continuously

Striving to feel above or superior to some other state or
    thing
By acting out what man is not,
And in doing so is actually inferior to all things
That act out only what they are or know.

Personality is true, like two times two
But the mistake in arriving at the answer three
Is in assuming it to be what it is not.
Personality is a habitual liar, for gain and no reason.
It promises today and regrets it tomorrow,
Finds comfort in shared tragedy instead of isolating
    sorrow in itself,
Surrenders its seat in a train
And the next day, well aware, is absorbed in a newspaper.
It gives with compasssion to someone in need
And five minutes later, well aware, pays no heed to a
    worthier case.
Or says it is sorry, I would if I could,
Well aware it would not.
What it loves dearly it will hurt cruelly
Appalling the knower at times with its viciousness.
It will stroke and console and gloat in maliciousness
Or writhe in regular remorse.

Personality is the tension of relationship
It acts out what man is not. Yet in acting it is true to
　　what it is:
A conflict of opposites that can never change
The source of frustration, worry and all bodyless pain —
Another form to be rid of by separation
By observation
By the knower seeing it for what it is,
Not him,
Without wasting time trying to change it, the
　　unchangeable.
That is self-knowledge
Wisdom.

What is the true and deathless part of man
This sun
That throws a twisted shadow of itself upon the earth?
Character. Man's character.
Not a caricature of character
That depends for its existence on wickedness and
　　adversity through which to shine.
Character is My sublime imprint on man's essence
His immortal consciousness,
The final form,

His function as an entity in the worlds below and above
Which in the shadow on the earth refracts to
    good and bad
Through the knower's limited knowledge of himself,
His inconsistency
Which is but to hold on to a world of unmoving opposites.
Consistency is an ever-moving thing
And so is character —
Consciously ever-serving, never-swerving from My
    wild wild will.
Man's gradual discovery of his character
(What a surprise it is, too)
Is the level of his undertanding
His longing and his loving through all his lives
And the mystery his million hearts have ached to solve.
Every character is different
Each a magnificent stamp of a man
If only the knower would look beyond the shadow
And find himself.
Man's character is an omnipotent omniscience behind
    his desire.
The arbitrator of the knowledge he choicelessly must
    seek as his interest or his love,

The co-ordinator of his life of relationship
The perpetrator of his suffering and his pain
The manipulator of his foolishness and his wisdom
The dictator of his every action —
His free will
His master
His Lord
And his God.

What is the essence on which man's character is
    impressed?

There is one essence and that is Me —
Consciousness, I or unity.
It is only on the step where man begins
That individuality of consciousness comes in.
This must not be confused with personality, mind or body.
They die.
Individuality of consciousness never dies.
It is the honey-hive. Inside.
You can experience it now within
As I exist or I am,
By being without thinking or knowing.

But busy mind quickly comes between with thinking

Making Me momentary

Which is a pity

For I am always here, inside.

I am a state at the end of knowledge

And no words can describe Me better than I am

Except, more simply, I.

I am at the edge of time

Being only now in this moment which is the last created
    thing —

And within you the only knower

When you are not knowing

Or are dead.

I am the end and beginning

Of inside.

This consciousness of mine is an unimaginable,
    ever-flowing, creator sun

Glaring blue-white

Through the pin-point archetypal patterns of
    character impressed on Me

(Indescribable Gods, far above even perfected man)

Which spread and diffuse their purity and image down
    through the worlds

In ever-widening spiral cones of form
Of diminishing intensity
And developing immensity of ignorance and multiplicity
    of purpose —
Complication.
These, my individual gods, altogether represent every
    variation and relation
That can occur in all the worlds.

So in summation
The vortex of man's character outside is the totality of
    all creation
Individual magnificence,
Inside unity of munificence
Me
The creator of the universe
For I and the Great God am one.

Earth man is no more important than the stone
Just a little nearer home for My Climber.
Stone is stone because it knows only what stone knows
And as it has no self-conscious mind
This knowing is preserved in the mind behind
In Consciousness.

A mind that dies could not run My mighty universe
For what would happen in between?
Selfish mind would forget
To keep the sheen upon the birds
And nudge the sleeping trees when spring has come.
This function I entrust to Consciousness.
Consciousness
Blue-white Consciousness.
Treasure-house of man's anatomy
All-seeing eye
Superlative intelligence.
Consciousness
Secret, sacred seminary

Gentle, elemental justice.

As each life recedes towards rebirth
Consciousness retains for man its seed and his most
  loved possession
His fancied knowlege, his unresolved impressions of
  what should and have been if . . .
And lays it like an unwrapped book
Unlived unread-dead
On a twisting, squirming, flaring fragment of desire to
  know or live
That on its own knows nothing and writhes in
  ceaseless impotence
Power denied an instrument
A laughing clown without a face.
Desire gasp-clasps this untried knowlege to itself in an
  orgasm of stuffing.
Filled and corrupt
It erupts
In boyish, joyous birth
A new entity, a new yearning, a new purpose
A new, eager, fool-fuel for the fire of life on earth
Whose own craving, still out of time, reaches along the
  line of now,

Divines the life to follow
Then plunges back into time
Forming a body, brain and mind
To accommodate its sorrow and evaporating happiness.

To crave for any state or object outside Me
Is an unconscious demand for disharmony,
Which is filled and stilled only in the pain of
     life-experience,
In the self-disintegrating realisation
That even if the object is attained
There is no gain that is not lost in death
Out there.

Living (not to be confused with Life) is disharmony.
Yet it is the taproot of the tree to Me,
For from each life there drips Inside
Into the immortal hive of each man
A distillate of understanding
An unconscious turning aside
A new kind of knowing of the form of life in which
     he hides
A new tuition, an intuition
A self-knowledge

A loosening from the form that ties him and denies him

A self-revealing, self-stealing knowledge

A whispering wisdom

Ageless

True.

And all the time, his curious, superficial mind gathers
	next-life's knowledge.

Only then, he will be strengthened again by his
	new-won understanding

Shining blue-white through his pain and wanting

Giving him a worthiness and depth indefinable

The noble and the lovable in man.

Consciousness

Keeper of the honey in all the hives

Deathless recorder of understanding.

Unerring justice.

What is this pearl, this understanding, whose price is
	measured in dead men?

He murdered my small daughter, the loathsome beast.

Look at him, chained to the dock, like the
	near-animal he is.

And the prosecutor points to my hollowed white face

Cave-eyed

Tear-dried

And says,

How much can a father hurt, who would deny such a
    tortured man his hate?

And I stumble to my feet, out into the street

Tears from a well I thought dry days ago

Streaming anew

Not for the little one taken

But for you . . .

You disgusting, repulsive, poor frightened beast

So bewildered that you cannot even remember the
    feast for which you now must pay

Except to know you did it

Though you truly didn't want to do it, though you did

And you would do it again, you know

If you should ever feel the same,

I know.

Yes, lock you up, you monster, for the man in you has
    transgressed man's law

And must be punished.

But I cannot lock you up inside of me with hate

For that would be to make you a part of me

And of that part I was freed many lives ago
When I, too, stood accused
Blinking, thoughtless and bemused like you, a
      near-ape mind in the body of a man
Learning to understand by undergoing.

How to understand death, without dying?
How to understand failure, without failing?
Today's accuser is tomorrow's accused
The slaughterer, the slaughtered
The fiend, the friend
The coward, the martyr
The brute, the God.
Thus does My highest Man look back on all with
      infinite understanding and compassion.
And therein lies the hope of bewildered beast
And shuffling, suffering man.

The process I have described of man's recurrence
Is the same for all form, sensible and insensible.
But as the senseless things cannot know pain
(The catalyst of understanding)
What is the link that keeps my endless chain
Endless

And consistent?

Pain is the self-conscious mind's apprehension of change.
Change is pain.
The unconscious man, like the metal, feels little pain
But his absent awareness does not affect the change.
My senseless things undergo infinite change without
surface mind to record the pain.
And the vapours of understanding or self-knowledge
that accrue
Are stored in the Climber,
Pieces of tomorrow's mind
Embryo of another you.

The key to this development
Is the final element to humble man who can be humbled.
His precious knowing for which he lives
And which in his conceit he imagines gives him
exclusiveness
Is nothing more to form below the level of the mind
Than heat.
Every change in form takes place in a new degree of heat
As every change in man takes place in
knowing/knowledge

Gained or lost.

Heat and knowledge are the same

As are change and pain

Except one is moving faster than the other further
   along the spiral

For steam is but excited water.

If stone is stone because My Climber there thinks he
   is a stone

What do you, My Climber, think you are

That keeps you from your own star

And bound to earth?

Do not attempt to answer for yourself — if you
   want the truth.

For what you think you are will answer

With all the vehemence and conviction that keeps you
   where you are.

The stone is equally as sure of itself.

To find the truth

You will have to look for the fact in Life

Where all truth is reflected without the need of opinion.

Obviously, what you really think you are will be

The thing best served by your life.

What is that?

You love your children and all the things you own,
Your honour, position and prestige,
Your money in the bank, your friends,
Even your responsibilities
And the little power you wield.
You tell what you love, by what you do not want to lose
And by the anxiety that afflicts you
When it is going or gone.
You do not cling to the match you strike
For that you recognise as life or living
An expendable necessity
Which, when kept to a conscious minimum, prudence
    terms economy.
You love all your things in varying degrees
And devote your life to their preservation
Or the accumulation of more of them.
Whatever is satisfied by such devotion will be what you
    think you are.

When man sends his child off to war, what then, does
    he love most?
His country, his precious way of life,

His duty, his principles, his responsibilities
Or his child?
Or does he love his fear that the boy or others might
hate him
Or denounce him, if he opposed unto death his
son's going?
Or perhaps it is his good name he loves?

The depth of man's love he knows only at the
moment of parting.
Let him choose which he would rather lose
His honour or his son
But only at the moment of parting.

Everything you love, treasure and fight for is outside,
Out there where your body can hug or caress it,
Out there, where your mind can gloat in the
knowledge you possess it
Or howl at the knowledge it is gone.
You, My Climber, live for and serve the body and
the mind.
You are trapped in the illusion of an individual good
outside,
Even though you know that all the possessors before you,

(Each one to himself the greatest good)
Still died to all he had.

Why does man desire to know anything outside himself?

He does not. Nothing ever tried harder to know itself.
But earth man is nothing more than a mass of
      knowledge of outside,
And in his desire to know himself he identifies with that
And toils relentlessly to gather more.
But pain and death and My consciousness finally
      save him —
And keep the Climber climbing
Towards the happy ending.

Do you see My great justice?

The treasured self-conscious mind of man that can be so
      clever,
Brilliant in one
And so unfairly dull and turbid in another
Has no knowledge of its own with which to answer the
      eternal questions.
It is a phenomenon of one short life

Whose expression is worldly knowledge.

What it expresses can be truth of a kind

Such as four plus one equals five

Without which there would be no world.

But it can never answer who you are

Or speak for Me.

Individual consciousness, the next form above mind, can.

Its realisation marks the birth of My Man.

This birth is but a shift of bias of knowledge, from outside

Where all is seen as individual

To inside, where all is seen as unity,

The crossing-point being a fixed degree of self-knowledge,

Of Me, My ways and My will.

So I climb the form in My staircase according to

    My knowledge of Me

And as much as I know Myself, there I'll be.

To unconsciously act out what you are not

Requires a special corrupting process

Familiar to man, as hypnosis.

You are hypnotised.

How else could you ever have stayed a tree, a dog?

Or not so long ago, even the man or woman you

    used to be?

Or now, even the man or woman you are?

I will explain,
But remember
You are the bodyless Climber who in fact knows all
But becomes entranced with the dazzling dance of each
    new form
And joins in
Forgetting you are hurrying home.

First, the hypnotist deprives the subject of his knowledge
By denying him deliberate access to memory
Through a state of trance, not unlike the dance of sleep
Into which all things sink so easily, rhythmically and
    thankfully.
This annihilates the personality
And leaves a still, thoughtless state of receptivity
For the hypnotist's suggestion to create a secondary
    personality
At any point at which he chooses to penetrate the
    memory,
Man being only what he knows.
Thus does the man get down on the floor and bark like
    a dog

When the hypnotist's suggestion reminds his memory of

This tiny, limiting piece of knowledge.

But as it is outside his own experience

The performance will be superficial

Absurdly unconvincing (to the dogs)

And to the audience rocking with hilarity,

But still a sincere, pathetic act by this grotesque pigmy of
    personality

Created out of his imagined knowledge

Of the intense living world of a dog,

Which can be reproduced only by the great
    primary hypnotist

Me

Who keeps you, My Climber, performing as an earth man

Until you wake up and see

Your own pathetic act.

When the barking fool on the floor

Realises he is man and not a dog, he stands up.

Not before.

POEMS OF
REALISATION
LOVE & NONSENSE

The climacteric of my life, the one amazing single event, was the Transcendental Realisation of Supreme Divine Being. This was done for me over a period of three weeks in 1968 in London. (In my lexicon, transcendental means that which transcends the senses.)

I owe the realisation to the presence of the divine spiritual master, the Blessed John, who came out of the deep unconscious of one of my students at the time (as intelligence miraculously enters the unborn child) and stayed for six weeks to teach me. The Transcendental Realisation was the culmination of his incomparable selfless gifts to me.

This poem describes this most rare of spiritual realisations. As the knowledge of it is beyond sense-perception, therefore beyond the scope of the rational or scientific mind, a degree of self-knowledge is necessary to relate to it. And I'd expect anyone who's moved to read this book to have that self-knowledge.

The amazing truth revealed in the realisation is twofold. First there is the revelation of aspects of supreme divine being and the immediacy of its presence which is completely undetectable by the mind and senses. Then the extraordinary revelation that love is the creator, and why love never gives up or tires.

As in all readings of truth, the usual error is in trying to make sense of it with the mind instead of simply getting the idea.

The Transcendental Realisation

Nothing.

Nothing but I.

Origin

Black, undistinguished, indistinguishable

Being Outside the world

Static

Forever aware

Forever

Forever present

Forever unformed

Forever unable to tell the secret of My being.

Yet, not from withholding

For I am Origin

Source

Beginning

Everness

Now

It.

Nothing.

I am producing Nothing.

And you, My Love,

Are producing Everything.

As Nothing

I am Supreme Being

Origin indescribable

No-suchness

A mystery

Of non-stirring, knowledge, ceaseless undetectable
    presence.

I am Origin of all action and sound

And My agency, the lesser being, the creator

Is Love.

Love is all.

Life is the action of Love

Love's business

The never-ending tireless endeavour to enact My Being

To describe with creation what I am

And lovingly creating what I am not.

Love fails.

Love always fails, yet never tires of failing

(Even now, Love groans at its own inadequacy to
    express in words the Truth I am.)

This the impossible, hopeless task of love
The reason why love lives to serve
Yet must forever remain sufficient only to itself, that task.
Love is the only means I have
And the only means to Me
Nothing.

I am producing Nothing.
An unimaginable substantive endingness
More real than even Love.
I am the space, the pause, the perimeter of sound and
    form.
I enable Love's beauty to be seen.
Where All and the Nothing meet is Man.

THE GARDEN

$\mathscr{C}$ome
I will show you a garden
Where nothing dies
My respite for you
When day is done.

Come, I will take you with me
Hold my hand
My love.

Precious, faintest, sweetest heart
Love's subtlety
Like purple dust
Afloat in light.

Elusive love lay in my heart
So light I felt it absent
So gentle sweet.

My pen as heavy as my words
Inadequate as my tongue

To name the namelessness of love.

Can I be so loved, so intimately, so divinely loved?
Is it possible for anything to care as much as love?

LOVE IS LOVE

Love must be free.

Must?

Well, love is free.

Free? Love is not free of free.

Sky is not blue of blue.

Sky is sky.

Love is love.

I mean, love must be free to . . .

Free to? You bind love to its freedom.

Free from . . .

Was love ever not free from?

Love is love. But what is love?

No, what cannot be love. Love is love.

Then love is speechless.

Ah, now you approach.

But now you limit love.

No, I limit you who speaks.

Then you must also limit I who act in love.

I do

For you would bind love to one action

And exclude love from another.

Then love is actless.

Ah.

But I feel love.

Then you would limit love to feeling.

What else am I for feeling is the end of me.

Yes, love.

THE MASTER'S SCORE

A screech, I am
Out of which
Life makes a melody.

Time-honoured am I
In my moment,
My brief place,
Scored by some Mozart
Somewhere
And played by the pangs and pains
Of the earth.

Screeching again I am
Abominable poetry . . .
But dare I,
Can I,
Judge the Master's Score?

NONSENSE

In the sweetness of the senses
Lies the Astral Confrontation
The Intellect-Dilemma
Of Non and Sense.

No one chooses Nonsense.
The Way is either Non or Sense.
No two ways about it.

This is a cow of a problem:
Two horns and only an animal brain between them!
That might be so if there was choice
But who would ever choose to be a cow
On the horns of its own dilemma, so to speak?

Non is the Way.
Sense is the Path.
To confuse them is Nonsense.

WHERE DO I STAND?

Oh, where do I stand
When I have no place to sit
And want no will to be
And wish that . . .
Wish?
I cannot wish nor want to be.
I go and come and pass.

ELEGANCE

*B*arry, my dear boy,
Let elegance in all things
And in all ways
Be your reminder of the good.

Elegance will unite your nature with your art.

As you take pains to search for right words
So take time to instil elegance
Into your demeanour, actions, speech and habits.

Change nothing. Be elegant.

ART

$\mathcal{I}$ live for art.
I feel the wisp of obliterating patience
In the irritation of my haste.
Art is the action of love
Love is the action of art.
Pressure is the time it takes for the two to melt together.

POOR MAN

King Midas poor man
Had a touch of gold
A gift of the gods
Turned sour.

I

I do not exist
But the existence of I is you
You do not exist
But the existence of you is me.
Without me there is no you
And there is no existence.
Except I.
Who do not exist.

YES, I REMEMBER

(Fishing alone in a rowboat at sea)

To find one moment explicit of the joy of life
To know the delusion of the joy of living
To watch terrified the sun sink at mid-day
From the bottom of a wave
To walk soul-footed as sunlight on the sea
Yes, I remember
I remember.

PALE FROG

*P*ale frog
Cramped still in tadpole garments
Waiting for the kiss of life
To turn you into Prince Charming.
Perhaps the wicked witch herself will die
And loose your spell
Or the maiden princess
Who shares your garden but fears the pond
May awake
Bathe naked
And smile just once in love and passing
At your uncomeliness.

THE SPIDER

The spider of emotion diligently spins her web
Urgently repairing every tear
That might reveal the truth
Since her life depends upon the web.
The web the mind
The spider the tireless emotion
Keeping mind intact
Against the piercing rips and tears
Of love and truth occasionally perceived
Revealing no thing (not even Spider)
Behind the web.

Web and spider
(horror of the pleasant walk through nature's garden)
Rise into existence
From that potent place of mind and self
Within us pleasant people.

Destroy not nature's spider or her web
They are but symbols
Of one mighty righteous whole

The garden of the earth.
Destroy instead
The spinner of all wickedness within
The spider of my self
That spins the web of anguish
And does not see the whole
The venomous humanised spider
Spinning inner dreams and dialogues
Of how the garden should be
Yet not daring to contemplate the hole
The exit from the web
Rent by love and truth
Lived.

Don't Pass Me By

*I*n the beggar's eye
In the furrowed brow
In the clenched fist
In the extended hand
See Me.
Don't pass Me by.

THE THRONE

Within this hulk of creaking flesh
A throne of light I've seen
And in it sits my own true self
With my beloved queen.
Though seeming two we are but one
As the petal is the rose . . .

CHANTICLEER TO THE I CHING

I come
With respect and love
Of truth and self-discovery.
No answer back am I
No echo
Just man
Pro tem
Until I find another name
Or it finds me.

Ancient oracle
Into the space
The pervading wisdom that separates and joins us
I now speak
Rejoin
To Top Line 9 of Chung Fu 61
Your admirable and respected response to my question.

I am Chanticleer
The plumaged voice
Trying to mount to Heaven

You say
Attempting the impossible, the absurd
And losing perilously
For how can the crimson crowing cock
Short in wing and stamina
Hope to fly so high?

Ancient oracle
Chanticleer does not crow for God
But for man
Does not attempt to fly
Except from peril
And then to the highest post or dunghill
There in inmost sincerity
With straining neck and strident call
Proceeds to draw attention to the dawn
Which indeed each day mounts to heaven
And sometimes carries with it
Awakened man.

THE FUZZ

We act for numerous conscious ends
Like a panoply of living hair
Each end having an illusionary end
Growing on and on
And on.
Whose is this head of pernicious restlessness?
Is this Medusa's hideous serpent wig?
There is no half to any hair
As there is no half to any longing.
Whose is this host body on which we grow
Towards countless fatuous ends
Before falling out?
Alas
We are the fuzz.

PIDDLING

I like to write poetry
Like small boys piddle in the bowl
Splashing my way to affect
Aiming low
And deep
So that no one in earshot can fail to hear
What's going on
Especially the proper people in the next room
Who have never piddled
Or cannot remember
The fun of crossed-swords
And public piddling.

GUILT IS GILT

*P*unishment and penalty are the gifts of the world
And only a fool does not accept his just rewards.

But guilt is gilt
Glamour
Slyly laid on the delicate lily
By self-offended hands.

Man
By choosing to be born
Out of the Hereafter into the Thereafter
Is patently guilty of the crime of self-projection.
The sentence is life
Ever recurring,
And the penalty is living through all its forms,
A justice we respect and love
As our survival.

But, here in the Thereafter
Man is found guilty of the same crime again

(An obvious injustice)
By himself and others.
Guilt is gilt
The golden god-calf of self-determinism,
Man's own glamorous image of himself,
Of what he should be, though is not,
And this he fretfully worships
In vanity and delusion.

Penalty and forfeit are not reasons for guilt.
They are the consequence of living,
The original error.
The sense of good exists in the exploitation of another
Somewhere
But guilt is the exploitation of one's self.

When penalty is inevitable, the pain is clean
And can be borne like life with a certain dignity.
But the pain of guilt
That self-inflicted injury
Can neither be borne nor erased.

Guilty I am of living.
Punished I am being.

The penalties and forfeits I accept.

But guilt is gilt

A self-made sentence

And I, for one, will not wear it.

NOTHING LEFT BUT LOVE

*W*hat does love want when first we love
That is so quickly sated?
Time together?
Or time to gather our senses,
More time to want outside of love?

And when the loving ceases
And the wanting begins and
One turns one's head away
Can love be gone?

May I always live with thee
And thee with me
And never know the difference.

BODIES

$\mathcal{B}$odies touching
Flesh between
Choral sounds of sweet lamenting
Always close, never near
Enough.

ETERNITY

Eternity is a place where things are themselves.
Eternity is when without the question mark.
I am Eternity.
You see and speak to my shadow.
My shadow, like yours, is a full-wound spring
Tensed with tomorrow on the fulcrum of now.
Release me, the despairing shadows cry . . .
Imagining that release means to die.
Not so.
Death is an ennobling thing,
Not the last tick of a run-down clock.
You are the tension, not the spring
As you are the shadow, not the thing.
Yet . . .

POOR FELLOW

You will not die when you die, poor fellow.
God, how I wish that you would.
Death is not won so easily.
The greatest good takes the greatest effort
And your clamour is to live in peace.
Die before you die
Or you will be stuck with yourself
Once again.
I have found death
But as the hunter not the hunted.

UP! CROCUS FLOWER

To Mark, my erstwhile step-son in England, on his
14th birthday

*C*ome August 2, 1975
I said we'd see the beginning of the end of you.
No pessimistic assumptions, please.
It's just that I perceived in March
The fibre of carnality withering your boyhood.
A year before I'd seen you heavy with the gross
    uncertainty of thirteen
The mien of failed old men called ungainly youth.
But shame, the quickening which age rejects,
The pulse of hope
Was in your eyes
As the first crocus flower must sense extinction
In the paradox of smothering snow.

Crossroads.
Oh Mark, which way for you?
How can you know the way is Up through snow and
    shame
When all the signposts point Across to journey's end?
Your mother knew,

Like mother Earth she mute-shouted
Up!
Up! Crocus flower
Up! Mark.

An April fire, I think it was,
Red with passion yet to come
Sparked the moment of genius in your mind.
Up it soared,
A poem flaring in the sacrificial groan of wood . . .
Your beginning.

I came across you once. You started, from your reverie.
I knew . . . this was where you spent your time: silent,
     gazing.
So March and April went
And I waited with mother Earth
To see what happens when the Crocus blooms.

Is it true that none of them survive?
Come August 2, 1975?

MY SON

I have glimpsed my Son behind the eyes of many men
The Son whom I shall never meet.

ETERNAL MOTHER, STRUGGLING SELF

For a woman who asked: What of my children?

*E*ternal Mother
Struggling self
Split with anguish and concern
At what must be
To heal the wounds
Of mindforms yet unborn.

Struggling mother
Eternal Self
How can the unforgettable be forgotten
When forgetfulness is unforgivable
Time's opiate?
Timeless you are,
Does such love as yours need words or thought-forms
The fancy necklaces of fear?
Are not pretty reassuring lights, kind words and
    admirable gestures
The cold comfort of sterile places and loveless
    homecomings?
The loving heart has not yet spoken
Nor thought

And never will.

Eternal Mother
Eternal Self
No threshold to your love
No end to your concern.
These children are love's idea
Your own creation
But not love's everlastingness which lies unsaid
Unformed
In your concern for them.
Hold this love in your being, not in your mind,

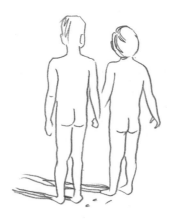

And it will speak for you mindlessly, timelessly
For it is this that makes the flower's fragrance
And bends the head that needs to smell.

Struggling mother
Your anguish is the right and wrong of doing what
    you must
That sacrifice of struggling self
To reveal Eternal Mother that you are
Eternal child that you cherish
Eternal Being
Among the silhouettes of parting and meeting.

OH, COPERNICUS

*16th century proponent of the heretical theory that the
earth revolves around the sun*

*L*ife by millennia
Revolved around Me like a sun
Awaiting Copernicus consciousness
To shatter my delusion.
I!
It is I
Who threads this blood-warm orbit
Round yonder heart of life
And endures its ever-swelling breeding, its
Corpuscular self-asserting waves
As my own guilt.
It is I!
Who is guiltless.
It is I
Who sags beneath the weight
Of vital gratification and greed
The sensuousness of
This dying sun
This life.
It is I misled by form

Who fancies the miasmic vapours
Of this bloody-red orbit
To be fineness of feeling
When I have no feeling
Only fineness.

Oh, Copernicus
Did you not guess that almighty sun is
Not so almighty after all
That together
Sun and I orbit a greater thing than life
An eccentricity
A void of unknowing, unfeeling
Far, far beyond life and sun at its deepest
Intimately present at its nearest
A fabric of senselessness and sense
Sleep, dream and oblivion
So fine as to have vanished
So subtle as to be absent?

Oh, Consciousness
You are the pristine presence I can never hold
The beauty I shall never knowingly express
In life.

Dying sun
Lord of all
That is hot and cold
You have outlived your lifefulness.
It is I
Consciousness
That now shatters your illusion.

BEDTIME

Let us retreat into the night
Where the long-nailed finger draws the line.

Let the light of the day
And the simplicity of sleep
Be run together, as water.
Let us drink
And, through the vapours of the skin
We shall serve the Presence and the Being
Of Unutterable Subtlety.

UNFOLD

*U*nfold
Let the bud become the flower
And the petals of the lotus
Fall supine
Upon the water.

Unfold
Let the being open
Beyond the close-scented cup of holding
So that only beauty's useless symmetry
Remains.

Are not dew and raindrops sweeter
Than sweat or tears?
Does the sun god taste the difference
Or even care?

Let the lotus life unfold
Let the pinched fingers of circumstance surrender
Fall back
In cyclic rhythm
On the palm that neither sweats nor weeps.

To the Blessed John

*B*lessed John
Your patient ache [*to visit India*]
Is but my knowing
That you are India.

Are you an ethic, you ask?
Yes.
Do you still love too much?
Yes. Thank God.

Blessed John
Your loving goes before you
Spills into the muck-raked vessel
And dissolves the crusting rings
Of self
And search.

Blessed John
Infinite poet
Humble craftsman
Unpretentious man

I would burden you with praise and love
If I could but find one spot in you
To lay them.

Let it be known
That the Blessed John is here
Hallelujah!
Hallelujah!
We are all saved
Again.

The postscript:

I have absorbed The Blessed John.
His passion is now mine.
Let his words be returned to the chaos.

I wrote John Hart (the Blessed John) a poem about death.
He replied saying it had 'tempted him to write a little
about life' and enclosed the following:

GREAT SPIRIT

O Great Spirit of the Earth
when I found you
I kept silence.
Now I will speak.

Ever creative of the Myriad Forms
Showered with light of the Mighty Sun and Sister Moon
Your exquisite absence of toil,
the life of mountains but a moment,
an ant's scrapings momentous.
A concentrate of Life Force,
disguised as disorder, on your Wanderings and Will we
    survive.

Your dust is our ancestor, our bones your food.
Sloth taught me existence as I trod on my way home.
propelled through the heavens.
You would tempt me to praise you, to be you,
to see
In the arms of a tree

The jump of a frog
That you were all, and excellence,
True Mother.

You would hold and deter, overawe,
and deep in the oceans,
a smile of a fish would register my toil and misery.

You are the same, but Great and Wise,
the web of your doings prolific.
You are but the gate, transparent, to form.
An idea, made abundant through Friction and longing,
a feast for the senses writ large in the sky,
telling all in your innocence.

You threaten the Fire, the Waters or Death,
Creation's shudder will fade you away,
delight take new fancies, and mountains subside like a
     breath.

Great Spirit live on, your formless, foodless belly in the
     Grand Idea,
smile as you shelter the blind, tremble at your terrors.
If your form defies you, it will not be,
you will be
at Peace.

WISE GUISE

To John (in reply):

*D*ear wise man writes of death and shedding form
Of the end of this travail
And all it does not mean.
And how well the master unpretentious poet puts it
Each phrase an artist's daub of coloured power
With not one mind-print to track him to his inspiration.
He speaks of death in deathless prose
An obvious deception.

But then he's mad
With a card or two in deadly prose to prove it.
You deathless ones are all the same
All mad.
You spend your days preoccupied with death-dealing
    introspection
While the life-short ones spend life-long days
Obsessed by living.
All mind.

In mindless madness
What I want to know is what is Life?

For all I see around me is living death
The form that I would shed
Or shred
The screams called people
The black hatred called night and mind
The wailing cry
The sob that rises to be understood
And chokes the child of understanding.

Mad poet
Are people people?
Or are people the form that we must shed
Death's nature
The image of illusion?

I suspect, mad poet that people are the Life-eclipsing
    moon,
That nearest, clearest, dearest and densest of the planets
Regaled in soft, alluring sentiment
Reflected light
Strung on threads of ragged steel
That rips the hand which cares
Enough to try to tear away the garment of delusion.
Deathless one

Mad poet
Pretentious you are after all
In your mind-guise of man or woman.

Illustrious trickster
With my bloodied, shredded hand
I salute you.

The following poem describes a realisation I had in 1978. Julie and I had recently moved to our new home in Highgate, London where I had started a new series of meditation meetings for men and women. This realisation happened a few weeks after I'd casually remarked to someone, 'I think I love my fellow man.'

THE BODY DIAMOND REALISATION

Still, the Blessed One retreats
And beckons me towards the Diamond Man
The incorruptible body of day and night
His.

Then
Through the Eye of Consciousness
I enter
A wisp of world
Within the Earthly world
A garden
A paradise
An Eden
Truly a State where Nothing dies
In the fullness of Love.

Then
The understanding that this is the Body of my
        Fellow Man!
Behind the brilliant diamond point
That only love of Him can bear, or dare, to enter.

And yet
Not mine, but Man's love it is
That has reduced me to the worthiness to love
For who loves who — and who is who
When in the Body of Mankind there is only I?
I am Blessed beyond all knowing except in the
     knowing of blessedness
That I am loved by Him — who I am.

This is the final humbling
To be loved by such a One as He
An unendurable delight, Ananda
That I can barely bear
And yet, to not bear it is to not deserve it
Impossible!
For such Blessedness is no gift, no reward
But the *means* of Love,
The diadem of Power Unearthly
The jewel untouchable by human longing
Set in Laurel-leaf upon the head
The Diamond Dew-point
The Jewel in the Crown of
Divine Consciousness.

SENSE THE BELOVED

Look at the trees
This is my sight
Smell the day
This is my fragrance
Hear the earth
This is my sound
Sense the beloved
This is my flesh
Taste the earth's produce
This is my fruit.

TO THE ROSE

*B*ecause I love the Father
I will not mourn your passing
But hand you back to Him
From whence you came.

VALE! JULIA

Written to Julie in 1982, the year of her death

$\mathscr{I}$ love the way you have with flowers
The sweetness that you bring to our home
And the wisdom that makes you truly great.

It is my privilege
To love you
Honour you
Cherish you
And respect you.

I am your loving husband
Who has no name
And needs none.

More often am I with you now
Than I have ever been.

TO MY AUNTS AND UNCLES

*I*t is not so much that I remember
But that I cannot forget
The kindness of you all
To my boyhood.

I hold each one of you
In my heart
Where memory is the sweet pang of love
Without image.

CONSCIOUSNESS

Consciousness is the abstraction of experience,
The realisation of phenomenal significance
In the absence of objective knowledge.

JADE

*T*rue woman of love and Consciousness
I would like to tell you
Why I named you Jade.

Esteemed by the ancient sages
for its soft lustre and arcane beauty
Revered and honoured beyond
the profanity of gold and sparkling stones
Is why I named you Jade.

Loving
Loyal
Willing
Caring
Nourishing when I was parched
Serving
Giving all to me and those I serve
And finally
The supreme surrender of your love
In love
To another.

That's why your name is Jade.

I loved you then.
And I love you now.

SARA

Beloved Sara
Gift of God
Incomprehensible beauty
Love of my life
God in woman
Thou art holy
And I am blessed.

DEATH

Death is not survival
Death is death.
Death is not a beginning
Nor an end.
Death is death.
Death does not exist.
Death is.
But the existence of death
Is life.

Index and Dates

The poems and songs in the book have been loosely arranged in chronological order with some variation.

The Work of Barry Long

Barry Long is recognised internationally as one of the leading spiritual masters of our time. His profound, vast and direct knowledge of life, love, truth, God and death has changed many thousands of people's lives. His uniquely practical, no-nonsense approach is appreciated in a world where religions, traditions and pseudo spirituality seem to lack the immediacy of true knowledge that can be really lived.

Barry Long addresses all aspects of life with the passion and clarity that enlightens and transforms what was dull and old into what is light and new. At the time of printing he is 76 years old. His best-selling books circulate in tens of thousands and his work is published in ten languages.

Although all of Barry Long's books and audio books are available from bookshops worldwide there are also a large number of audio and video recordings of his meetings that are only available by mailorder from The Barry Long Foundation. A catalogue of his work will be supplied on request.

On two of these audio cassettes (only available from The Foundation) Barry Long reads some of his poems from this book:

Songs of Life

Most of the songs from the *Songs of Life* section

Barry Long's Epic Spiritual Poems

The poems from the *Epic Poems of Truth* section

OTHER BOOKS BY BARRY LONG

BARRY LONG'S AUTOBIOGRAPHY is due to be published shortly

A PRAYER FOR LIFE
The Cause and Cure of Terrorism, War and Human Suffering

A spiritual master's perspective on why our civilisation is being shaken and where humanity makes its mistakes – and his prediction of the outcome. This is a plea for us to wake up to the appalling truth of our situation, and to the human condition that unknowingly perpetuates suffering and misery while devoutly wishing and hoping for change. Barry Long demonstrates the way each individual can contribute to a new life on earth.

'Clear, precise and very direct. Highly recommended.' GOLDEN AGE

THE WAY IN – A book of self-discovery

A revelatory book, uncompromising and profoundly powerful in delivering the truth. It shows how to avoid the pitfalls and delusions of the spiritual path, and how to reach the ultimate truth for ourselves. This is a survey of the entire process of spiritual realisation – placing the whole responsibility on the individual, with no intermediary belief systems. This is the most complete statement in one volume of Barry Long's teaching. A great source of inspiration and self-discovery.

'Immense insight into the truth within us.' GOLDEN AGE

THE ORIGINS OF MAN AND THE UNIVERSE
The myth that came to life

This work of immense vision tells the whole story of how we and the earth got here – from the Big Bang to the coming End of Time. It relates our inner life to the outer world in ways that draw us deeper into a solution for the ultimate question, the one that every human being has asked down all the ages: What is beyond the heavens? What's behind it all? What on earth are we doing here? A book capable of changing your picture of the world forever.

'A profound and spellbinding book by one of the world's greatest masters. This book is destined to become a classic.' THE PLANET

MAKING LOVE – Sexual love the divine way

This book offers a life-changing encounter with real love; a way to keep love constantly fresh and alive through honest, pure and conscious lovemaking. This is a unique and radical tantric teaching that transforms your relationships and brings the dream of true love closer to reality. It gives lovemaking its due place in the spiritual life. Essential reading for anyone who is serious in the search for real love.

A landmark bestseller, this book has transformed the love-life of thousands worldwide.

Also available on audio tape.

'The most profound insights on love and sexuality that you are ever likely to encounter.' NEW AGE GUARDIAN

KNOWING YOURSELF – The true in the false

A collection of observations about life, truth, love and death made while the author was undergoing an intense process of self-realisation. These fresh, clear, challenging insights are a map for us as we follow our own spiritual journey into self-knowledge. As you read you discover the difference between love and emotion, joy and sentiment, your will and your desire, and you see what lies behind all human motivation.

'A book to be highly recommended.' YOGA TODAY

ONLY FEAR DIES – A book of liberation

This is a book of essays on the causes and effects of unhappiness and the spiritual process of 'dying for life'. It shows us what we can do to release ourselves from the tensions of living, and challenges us to give up our 'right to be unhappy'. The perspective then shifts to the world scene – helping us to disengage from the mass delusions of the human condition.

'A wake up call.' MAGICAL BLEND

WISDOM AND WHERE TO FIND IT – A book of truth

In self-discovery we question life's purpose and our relationship to wider society. This book tackles some of the vital questions: What is 'good'? What is truth? Why does mankind suffer? Do we really have control over our lives? Why am I alive? It teaches self-observation in a way relevant to ordinary life.

'Ideal introduction to the teaching of Barry Long.' SCIENCE OF THOUGHT REVIEW

MEDITATION – A FOUNDATION COURSE – A book of ten lessons

A no-nonsense practical course which is very clear and easy to follow. Step by step you learn to still your busy mind and learn how to deal with worry. The concise lessons give practical exercises you can use at home and at work. It is free of esoteric or religious overtones. This is practical, effective meditation and puts you on the road to a more harmonious, fulfilling life.

'One of the most practical guides to meditation on the market.'
NEW AGE GUARDIAN

STILLNESS IS THE WAY – An intensive meditation course

This book is an inspiring guide to self-knowledge, in the form of an intensive three day course. It takes us through the restlessness and confusion often encountered in spiritual practice and goes beyond the formal devices of sitting meditation. It introduces us to a state of consciousness in which we may live more freely and naturally where words such as truth, love and grace are no longer abstractions but living reality.

'It is thrilling to discover a reliable guide on this path of meditation. Barry Long is a remarkable teacher whose words have the certainty of a deeply realised being.' MEDITATION MAGAZINE

RAISING CHILDREN IN LOVE, JUSTICE AND TRUTH

This is a compendium of advice given by Barry Long to parents who have asked him for help in handling family relationships.

It is largely a book of dialogues, grounding the spiritual dimension in actual case histories. The very many topics cover familiar domestic situations as well as more difficult problems. *'Parents looking for a spiritual guide to raising their children need look no further than Barry Long's extraordinary book. You are in for an invigorating journey, face-to-face with one of the world's most direct, simple spiritual masters who also happens to know about paying the bills every month!'* NATURAL PARENT

TO WOMAN IN LOVE – A book of letters

A book of letters about love, its pain and transcending beauty, written by women of all ages from many countries to a man who offers the purity of a divine love beyond personal considerations. Barry Long's replies are intimate, challenging, compassionate letters to Woman, his beloved.
'A work of honesty and love that will speak to many.' ADYAR BOOKNEWS

TO MAN IN TRUTH – Enlightening letters

This book is a selection of letters to Barry Long from men endeavouring to live the spiritual life. The letters and replies are testimony to the sometimes agonising inner conflict that men experience between the inner drive towards truth and the pressures of living and working. Always revealing, Barry Long's answers are incisive, compassionate, practical and profound.
'Long speaks about how love can be used to strengthen each man's connection with the great mystery.' CONSCIOUS LIVING

Barry Long Audio Books

Start Meditating Now
A Journey in Consciousness
Seeing Through Death
Making Love
How To Live Joyously

Barry Long's books and audio books are available from bookshops or from The Barry Long Foundation.

Contact Details

For further information on Barry Long and a catalogue of his current books, tapes, videos and teaching program contact:

The Barry Long Foundation International
A non-profit charitable organisation

Australia ~ Box 5277, Gold Coast MC, Queensland 4217

England ~ BCM Box 876, London, WC1N 3XX

USA ~ Suite 251, 6230 Wilshire Boulevard,
Los Angeles, CA 90048. *Or call* 1 800 4971081

Email ~ info@barrylong.org

Current details of Barry Long's work along with statements, articles and biographical information can be found online at:

Website: ~ www.barrylong.org